THE SORROW WE BORROW

POOJA Prem MEHTA

BLUEROSE PUBLISHERS
India | U.K.

Copyright © Pooja Prem Mehta 2024

All rights reserved by author. No part of this publication may be reproduced, stored in a retrieval system or transmitted in any form or by any means, electronic, mechanical, photocopying, recording or otherwise, without the prior permission of the author. Although every precaution has been taken to verify the accuracy of the information contained herein, the publisher assume no responsibility for any errors or omissions. No liability is assumed for damages that may result from the use of information contained within.

BlueRose Publishers takes no responsibility for any damages, losses, or liabilities that may arise from the use or misuse of the information, products, or services provided in this publication.

For permissions requests or inquiries regarding this publication, please contact:

BLUEROSE PUBLISHERS
www.BlueRoseONE.com
info@bluerosepublishers.com
+91 8882 898 898
+4407342408967

ISBN: 978-93-5989-476-8

Cover design: Abhijeet Pradhan
Typesetting: Tanya Raj Upadhyay

First Edition: October 2024

dedicated to

the heart that feels

and the soul that reveals

TABLE OF CONTENTS

CANVAS 1
WONDER BLUNDER 2
MOMENT 4
PALMS 5
THIRST 6
PRISONER OF PAIN 7
HOW PROFOUND 9
WAR 10
FOUND AND LOST 11
LOST GAME 12
LONELY MIND 13
DEATH 14
INNOCENT SIN 15
GIRL CHILD 16
BURNING HUMANITY 17
SULKING SUN 18
BONDAGE 19
SILENT SALUTE 21
SURVIVAL 22
IMAGES… WORDS… VOICES 23
AFTER LIFE 25
LOVE BLEEDS 26
HIGH 27
SO DEEP 28
ON SALE 29

ROSE	30
BELONG	31
A BEGGAR	33
VIOLENT VOID	34
LOST CHILD	35
MAYBE… MAYBE NOT	36
RISING	37
HOPE	38
UNCONSCIOUS BLISS	39
ONE MOMENT	40
HOLLOW SKY	41
WRITER'S LAST WORDS	42
PRAYER	43
LOVE	44
FLIGHT OF LIGHT	45
THY FATHER	46
KNIFE	47
SOULLESS SPELL	48
INSANE VOID	49
BECKON ME	50
MOON	51
SUNSET CALLS	52
THIRTY SECONDS	53
WILD CHILD	54
GOD & MUSIC	55
LAST FLIGHT HOME	57

CANVAS

A Collage of memories fear death
As I move on to sketch new beginnings
The canvas cries
I bleed as the paint dries
Tormented by the painter's lies

The painter can't fathom his art,
defying his own heart
His mind races faster than his subconscious can
Solitude is his disease and his sweet solace too
Failed self-preservation of so many years
His own tears he deeply fears

Both his lover and shadow abandon his colours
Penetrating the blacks of his own creation.
Questioning himself, his Art
and Life's greater intention.

WONDER BLUNDER

Why do the most beautiful things in life hurt,
I wonder
The ecstatic rain drops that bring the thunder
The perfect love kiss that now seems like a blunder
The delivery of a beautiful child
Who grows and goes wild

The mysterious glimmer in your beloved's eyes
That cover and hide forbidden lies
The love that the almighty gives you
For all the sins he almost forgives you
To the sun that fades when you breathe your last
To all the times you died while exploring this life
so ruthless and vast
To the ones you forgot along the way
Faces you leave behind in ignorance and dismay
Why do the most beautiful things in life hurt,
I wonder
The ecstatic rain drops that bring the thunder
The perfect love kiss that now seems like a blunder

PENNILESS PAIN

Formless figures unknown to my mind
Whirling their way to make me see
How they glare at me

They judge my every move
Stare in my eyes and laugh at my torn shoe
I am a specimen for the world that does not know
One day God was on the street and felt this low
In the queue they find me too slow
So they push me and that's the final blow

Cursed by heaven is poverty
To be treated as dead while you still breathe, sheer brutality
Amputated for the world, a destitute they don't need
Somewhere even God believes he planted the wrong seed

Dark skies, Priest lies, Humanity dies.

MOMENT

Who are you but a star in the soft sky
What are you but a whisper in a lullaby
Hold the moment…hold it close
Live the laughter before it goes

Smell the roses loving the thorns
Say you know the place we belong
Finding each other in each other's songs
We carry on holding on…

Who are you but a star in the soft sky
What are you but a whisper in a lullaby
Hold the moment…hold it close
Live the laughter before it goes

Dreams that will sting you will finally bring you
Bliss that befriends you as life rolls on
Courage to smile when others offend you
Knowing you know the feelings
that lay in your bed are so strong

Who are you but a star in the soft sky
What are you but a whisper in a lullaby
Hold the moment…hold it close
Live the laughter before it goes

PALMS

The thin lines, the unseen scars
The unknown magic, the thirsty mars
Beckons the insanity in every man
Facing mountains, Biting sand
Life stands unnoticed as I pass it by
Without looking in its eye
Covering my sins with a lie
Still desiring to fly

I write a word
A story of glory, of bliss
If we've not heard, we cannot miss
The sign of madness, the passion behind the pain
The innocence behind the insane

THIRST

Innocence gets crucified a little every day
The purposeless grin that curved my lips does not form so effortlessly today

The charade, the facade, the trade called love is no longer available for the deserving

It was sold in the market of life last night

As she touched him
Could any hell be worse
Where there is no passion, only thirst

PRISONER OF PAIN

The wounds of yesterday bleed away
as I lie in blissful numbness
that stares, that screams
It's an alley of nightmare and a lane of dreams

I am a prisoner of pain
I am the wetness in the rain
I am a leopard, I am the lame

Wounded he cries out to his God
Draped in regret, he lies down on a sword
The words that kill him are the words he wrote
Unending bondage of a wounded soul

I am a prisoner of pain
I am the wetness in the rain
I am a leopard, I am the lame

Sirens of insanity, curses of lust
Perception blurred; darkness stirred
The vacuum that crawled in my bed tonight lies motionless now
The refuge of your touch comes back to me somehow

I am a prisoner of pain
I am the wetness in the rain
I am a leopard, I am the lame

HOW PROFOUND

How profound was your love I wonder
Sharp and strong like a sword
Or weak and soft as a feather
Fickle yet real as weather

How profound was your love I ask
Deep and dry as still water
That kills me with every drop
Refusing to flow in me anymore

How profound was your love I plead
That leaves me at the mercy of wind and storm
Which used to cover me in cold nights and kept me warm

As our love lies motionless in your barren eyes
I search for meaning in the bare skies
That beckon me to stay and still push me away

WAR

Are we masters of our destiny
Or the reflections of a country

The blind patriotism of man
awakened by the divine death of a newborn

They lost more men than we

That is our trophy

FOUND AND LOST

Round and round I hit the ground
Feeling passion and pain that has no sound
Lost and found, Lost and found

Thoughts that sail beyond me
Desires that fail to perish
Hiding under my mortal skin
Scars that I deeply cherish
Tearing me, scaring me to find the unknown at any cost
Found and lost, lost and found

The maze, mystery and myth unfold
The love story was finally told
Feeling passion and pain that has no sound
Give me a dream so profound
Lost and found, I hit the ground

Innocence that remains
Calling out a distance name
Agony or Ecstasy, both fleeting flames
Who holds the pulse, who feels the shame

Ending this blame game, I stand before myself
Found and lost, lost and found
Round and round I hit the ground
Feeling passion and pain that has no sound

LOST GAME

When the sword of love strikes
My conscience bleeds from the scattered memories
That now seek refuge from shame

Shame that they failed to live forever
Glory for the time they breathed like moments

The seed of betrayal is sown
Who will bear this burden of a wounded heart?
If this was predestined from the start
Then God was a player, my life was a dart

LONELY MIND

The nightmares that crawl into my bed
Are the dreams that danced in my eyes one night
I bare them as a burden, what once seemed like bliss
Only to find life a little more amiss

The betrayal of love, the wicked hands of time
Are the treasures of a broken heart of mine
In the palms of my hand, I see a sign
Sorrow of an unforgettable kind
You can find in every lonely mind

Perhaps tomorrow the pain will subside
As he silently contemplates suicide
Unable to hide from the harsh tide
That ruptured innocence with everyday lies
A vacuum that has now filled weeping skies.

DEATH

They say I conquered; they say I lived
I say I crawled
I say I fibbed

They say it's morning, they say it's day
I say it's a lonely moon shying away

They say it's over; they say it's death
I say it's a promise which had to be kept

INNOCENT SIN

The blood of innocence bursts through the shallowness of age
Is it the sweet whisper of Satan
Or the call of a distant sage

The rage of life engulfs me as I lie naked with fear of the next word, that will kill me
The last sleep beckons me as I fight to live
To take, to give

A hollow past, an impure present and a petrified future we seek
But it all looks quite bleak

Sing no more says he
For a heart without his light will not kneel at his altar
He who lives in innocence will not falter

GIRL CHILD

When did conception turn into deception
The child they conceived together
They deceive now in the dark
God sheds a tear seeing man's pointless fear

While the palms unlearn the known,
love lies enslaved in the hands of the cruel
As silence cries for the child who lost her mind
She now lay next to the dead womb
Motionless yet gravely alive

Why then in her grave she still craves
The belonging she did not feel
The wounds she could not reveal
She's a girl, is that a raw deal
A girl could be a goddess in progress
or maybe a prostitute in distress

Alas we'll never know what mystery she had to show
Her voice silenced before she could speak
Has man reached insanity's peak
Or are we just soulless people suspended
Waiting for something more to settle the birth score

BURNING HUMANITY

I surrender to the merciless killing of mankind
Where can we see, where can we find
Humanity that is so blind

That searches, that seeks
That crumbles, that's weak
What a façade of aimless words

A collage of unending sins that die in front of your naked eye
Draped in a meaningless sigh

Give me the sun that spreads faster than the fire that now burns my face surviving this pointless race
Where the winner loses it all
While the looser is made to look so small

SULKING SUN

I saw the sun dying today
He said he was tired of rising to a world that did not care
Who live aimlessly not knowing that I burn myself in every way
To just give them a better day

I bare their marks, hear their remarks
But I glare it away thinking they'll love me someday

I never resist or give up
For to leave my beloved in darkness I do not know
Even though my love I do not show

Now I lie tired waiting for a smile
I seek eyes that do not turn away
That can see me for me
Not a part of forgotten glory
Or a part of a text book story.

It's a lonesome price to pay for immortality
Burn away with me tirelessly says he
As I continue to exist in agony
Though it means nothing to many,
sometimes not even to me

BONDAGE

To dwell in a quiet corner for the things that passed her by
Was not a privilege she had
The crushed innocence
The suppressed smile
The wicked times
The forehead lines
They spoke as she sat in silence
Eyes screaming
Freedom… Freedom… Freedom One Day

WANDERING SHADOWS

I will not submit nor surrender to the wavering fickle mind
Instead, I seek to find the unknown that whispers, that screams
A heart that survives yet dreams

The changing lines of my forehead crippled with time
The warm hands of a weeping mother holds on to a hope, that will help her believe
That the lamp she lit will burn long after she leaves

With every bondage why is there pain
Why every discovery makes me more insane

Where the will to live seems to be in vain
Is there anyone who stands to lose or gain?

SILENT SALUTE

Draped in insanity, overwhelmed by senseless humanity
I search for a sign
A name, a road

One that I can walk on without a doubt
One where I can talk without a thought
One that cannot be sold or bought

A life that seeks shelter in the eyes of the found
One where silence is more profound than sound.

SURVIVAL

The Destined Death of the Divine Soul
Drapes itself with treasures of Lust,
 of Love, of Passion, of Pain
I crawl beneath my own Skin afraid to look within

The frail conscience hangs itself
Spirit dies, man remains
Living with a frivolous name
Flaunting his feared fame

What a Shame

This Survival Game.

IMAGES... WORDS... VOICES

They run to me as they make wake way to stay
Late in the night and wake up with me on a bright

hot day
In every form and way
When skies are both blue and grey
Images, Words, Voices surround me every minute of the day

I gather them every place I go
Every fair, every funeral
Every name, every nation
They never cease to indulge in the mystery of madness
Or dwell quietly in the loud corner of sadness

Images… Words… Voices

Drills
Kills
Lives
Gives
Shivers
Quivers

Like a mirror
Like an illusion
They hide, they disguise
They breathe, they lead
To see the missing key
It's about you, it's about me

The silence of the soul
The reason behind the role
Images, Words, Voices
Soothe the chaos they create
Surviving race and time
Moving past raging crowds,
Living in distant clouds
Images… Words… Voices
Images… Words… Voices

AFTER LIFE

The eyes of the blind, the ears of the deaf
Are precious to the ones that can see the undefinable

Who can hear this silence?

Who can seek the unfindable?

Who can feel the unknowable?

Who can move when others stop

Who can live when the body will drop

LOVE BLEEDS

What is this emotion called love?

It's the inspiration of a poet
It's the roar behind a riot

It's the treasure of a painter
It's the pride of a banker

Hunger, lust, fear are its precious pearls
The hearts they walked on are their cherished crowns

A game for many
Death for a few

Constantly on its knees it begs for mercy

What in the name of love have we done

Captured the freedom of a loved one
And killed the spirit of a rebellious son.

HIGH

What kills me is not the ones that went away
I fear those who I see everyday
Who are these faces
What do they want
They injure me with a smile and a taunt

What is a blessing
What is pain
Without the dark clouds where is the rain

With every joy there is sorrow
We hold on thinking of a better tomorrow
It comes and passes us by,
while we lie in the midst of chaos letting out a sigh

Give me a high
Just one high before I die

SO DEEP

In your silence I sleep like a baby
In your absence I feel incomplete
I promise you I don't want to fall in love
but it happens when I enter so deep

Don't hold your breath
Don't leave the stretch
Just look at me
Tell me you know on this tropical day
we'll create some snow
In your silence I sleep like a baby
In your absence I feel incomplete

Sweep me up in the morning light
Descend not even when the dusk settles the
destiny dust between us
Do I see a part of me in you or did I just believe
Your presence deepens with every hello
I promise you I don't want to fall in love
but it happens when I enter so deep

ON SALE

As she lies there shaken and skinned
Bleeding of the life she once embraced
Her origins cannot be traced
Her soul could not buy her food
So she stood there to be bought and sold
By a saint or a sinner
By a fascist or a fool

ROSE

Every rose has a thorn, it's written, it's told
A sentence so bold today I behold in awe

Aimlessly dwelling on a path, I did not pave
Only for love every soul craves

It evades him calmly as he wallows on
Always in self-pity, sometimes in self-pride

Everyone is destined to bleed with a kiss or a knife
Foolishly he hides from this incarnate truth of life

Relentlessly to prove our rhythm
My truth I can barely fathom

How much of my skin shall be ripped
As we painfully accept this God gift

Every rose has a thorn, it's written, it's told
A sentence so bold today I behold in awe

BELONG

I could go on singing a song
What was right about us
And still what went wrong

I could pretend I don't care
The lies you told lie before me bare
Knowing we were not meant to be
But still, I can see you belong to me

You belong to our mornings
You belong to our dear pain
You belong to our laughter
And that beautiful walk in the rain…

Why do I linger on your every thought
I felt a piece of heaven open in me when we met
Still there are parts about us I just don't get
Will destiny unfold its wings
And you'll fly to me

I could pretend I don't care
The lies you told lie before me bare
Knowing we were not meant to be
But still, I can see you belong to me

You belong to our mornings
You belong to our dear pain
You belong to our laughter
And that beautiful walk in the rain…

Sending a prayer, I look up at the sky
Forgetting it would mean
I would have to wilfully die
Staring at your goodbye note
The night is still waiting to cry

I could go on singing a song
What was right about us
And still what went wrong

A BEGGAR

They pass me by
Every single day

They fear thee
But can't see
I am reality

I seek bread
How ignorant of me!

VIOLENT VOID

The rebellious lines swindle a few deals
Life turns a corner
I break a leg

Sorrow rises like the tide
Feeling hollow inside
I seek refuge from it all
Bondage both great and small

Pain I hide from follows me in the alley of my mind
I hide behind
It crawls beside me
Silently screaming
Emptiness
Without doubt
Is what life is about
So why cry out

LOST CHILD

Come to the rescue of this lost child
Does he stand a chance in this jungle of wounded souls?

Will he be standing in solitude weeping, helpless?
Working for water and success

Does he stand a chance in this cocoon of conceit?
Can he climb his way without crime or deceit?

A fleet of tamed blinded calves
Building our way through our worst halves
We seek to find with an evil mind
But a good heart cannot be bought
Maybe that's what humanity forgot.

MAYBE... MAYBE NOT

She said to him injured in both heart and soul
If you leave, I will die
He thought it was a dramatic lie
So, he left anyway and flew far to a new land

The remorse was too much for her to bare
Her reality exceeded despair
She made up her mind to see it as her end

Why I wondered
Could I have changed that
Maybe... Maybe not

Someday in the liberation of death they will live together, she believed
Maybe...Maybe not

RISING

As he rose on the third day
I attempt to rise once in a lifetime

Only to see myself still more beneath my best

How much do I have to fall
To rise again

HOPE

Where can I find refuge from rebellion?
When will I find solace in my soul?
The stagnant growth of insane pain
But I still enjoy the rain that burns my face

I look at the mirror that reminds me of a man I could be
The life that I can see
The magic I could make
If I could give up being fake

I reject the acceptance I'll never get
I avoid what I can't forget

To live without a reason
There is no bigger treason

UNCONSCIOUS BLISS

Love is for the senseless who won't want anything from a touch

Like a child that seeks refuge in his mother's bust
Pure hunger, no lust

Just a thoughtless act of craving for the one
Like he wants the rain from the sun

A squirrel seems to know her purpose unconsciously
The bird embraces its wings with delight
Why man fights with all his might
Unable to still never get it quite right

The drapes of bliss are thorns in disguise
Is there ignorance in the wise
Wrath in mother nature's eyes
Knowing man's greed for more will never suffice

ONE MOMENT

I forgot the way you smelt the night you met me
I forgot how you moved the first time I saw you

I forgot when you gave me a lifetime in just one moment

HOLLOW SKY

Whose face stares at me from the hollow sky
They entice me with a smile, kill me with a high
A universal religion is suspended like a lie

Consumed with excessiveness, he searches for bliss
He pays the price for falling in love
Accepts it as a curse from above

WRITER'S LAST WORDS

A writer was found hanging off a fan that night
Words that were written were not quite right
Life had not taken a natural climax
The half-burnt candle bled with wax

The ink is still wet from the last piece she wrote

It had a quote…

Do not turn me away the way the world has
Accept me thee, let me live without agony.

PRAYER

Fill me with the silence that surpasses words

Engulf me with the warmth that precedes harshness

Embed in me a heart that feels the fear of the lame

Carry me in your sacred eye that will blind me from sorrow

Drape me with a story which unfolds your glory

So one day I can find

A Panasonic Mind of a Divine kind

LOVE

I fall in it and then I rise from it

Love.

That's what they call it

FLIGHT OF LIGHT

Light draws me as I try to find the key to eternity

The close disappears and merges
The new too dissolves

Out of words, deep with fear I dwell in silence
Trespassing this life and next

How much can I run
Can I escape a rebirth?
If not
Let me stand still and obey his will

THY FATHER

Strange suspicions, unknown truths seek an answer
I hear a prayer

He kneels, I shiver

I thought he knew; he thought I did

Strangers to each other's minds we embrace

Our souls one, our ways differ

God and me to I refer

KNIFE

Life is a knife with two sharp ends
It makes you bleed; it makes you plead
It makes you run; it makes you burn in the sun
Your skin peels mercilessly, your conscience takes disguise
You don't know whether you are a miserable fool or outrageously wise

Where does the story end the actor asks
Tired of wearing a million masks
Where can I bury myself
In a warm lap or a grave gap

It's a jungle of confusion
Which may never give us a solution

But the journey has its moments
It's a small price for the high that makes you fly
That will carry you till the day you die

SOULLESS SPELL

Insanity beckons
 the brave
the soulless lead the world

A story without a beginning
A tale that never ends
The journey of lust that breaks to join.
Join to break, yet again

Sorrow, Search, Shame
Stand dumb founded at the merciless existence of man who lies at the feet of a vengeful woman

Can there be a more gruesome union but of two empty minds
Lust, a destruction of a supreme kind.

INSANE VOID

He looks at me with a question
Unable to understand his intention
I blindly exist in a world of possession
that reeks of deception

Echoes of lies that fly behind my eyes
Sink into a deep sleep of depression

The answer still hangs unanswered
The warrior still stands unconquered

He dwells deep in empty sounds
Insanity can make a man tread new ground

BECKON ME

My mind drips of his name
His stained glory screams from the roads
Distorted people, dejected souls
I feel smaller than the smallest

I lose grip of sanity
As reality fights fate
Open the gate
Rescue me

Captured by it all
I stand still, yet crawl
As I wait for my final call

MOON

Fatal truths surround us and we look away
The darkness of the night scares me as much as the surviving day
Why not wash away the past that seems too vast
Almost like a religious overcast

We betrayed him when we were born
We forsake him as we die
Through a fact and a lie
They are mere interpretations of a lost truth
As simple, as uncouth

So close to life yet so far
Now I understand why every moon has a scar

SUNSET CALLS

When sunset calls and the night falls
Will you be there
Will you see it was meant to be
Travelling miles, destiny smiles
As we capture the beauty within and without
I call out to you in my dream
Your memory whispers and screams

The breeze that caressed your hair and face
Made me see the forgotten beauty of life
Your eyes reflect my lost innocence
The beauty I feel in your presence
Divinity fills up my sky
I call out to you in my dream
Your memory whispers and screams

How you see through my charades and lies
When did we get beyond distance and time
Your voice lingers deep in my every word
I seek shelter in you like a free bird
Are you the missing piece of my soul

When sunset calls and the night falls
Will you be there
I call out to you in my dream
Your memory whispers and screams

THIRTY SECONDS

I asked him if he'd been crushed
One day he sighed
She walked away, voice echoing
Say what you want to say
You've got your last thirty seconds

A lioness ripped his heart apart that night
It was quite a sight
As the light went out, he had no doubt
Thirty seconds was what life was all about

As she lay in the naked arms of a stranger
Her tender virginity was in obvious danger
In the business of flesh
Thirty seconds is all it takes for innocence to break

When death smiled at him from a distance
He embraced it in an instance
He was a victim of evil circumstances
but like life, death gave him no chances
They left him aimlessly to wander and wonder
Was loving her his destined joy or his greatest blunder.

WILD CHILD

The Sound of music resurrects itself when the intellectual sleep
Rebellion forms with the birth of a child
The vibration of which is subtle and mild
Was he born to be drifted and wild
When Intellect rises, he knows that the sound of innocence may be muted with time.
No melody or mystery will we ever find with a chaotic mind
He finds himself drowning in self-doubt as the words almost form
Who is the dictator, what is the norm
As I fly inward to find the freedom to feel if not say
Is the wild child slowly fading away

GOD & MUSIC

They said
Music will set you free
Let you be you
Let me be me
They said
Music will fill your soul
Could be country, jazz or rock and roll

Let me be with my music
Let me be with God
Let me be with my music
It will hold me when all else will fall

The kaleidoscope of notes trickle through me and give me joy
Life is a series of events, to some merely a free toy
The fragments of sound move around us
Healing the pieces that lie within us broken

Let me be with my music
Let me be with God
Let me be with my music
It will hold me when all else will fall

The continuous flow of energy and vibes
Rhythm that travels through countries and tribes
I wake up with a song from my own jukebox
Hoping to find my dreams that I found and lost

Let me be with my music
Let me be with God
Let me be with my music
It will hold me when all else will fall

LAST FLIGHT HOME

Laughter fades to black as colours smile in a restless void
To swim beyond the sea
To exist beyond life
To fly beyond the wind
I seek an answer in the eyes of a stranger
Love fears no danger
Hits and misses
Tears and kisses
Leads to heaven and hell
As the dew clears, I see reality that stares at me
Come to death with a smiling face no matter what it takes
For you and your God's sake.

www.ingramcontent.com/pod-product-compliance
Lightning Source LLC
LaVergne TN
LVHW041635070526
838199LV00052B/3370